TEEN
SURVIVAL
GUIDE

SURVIVING
A FIRST BREAKUP

SHERRI MABRY GORDON

Enslow Publishing
101 W. 23rd Street
Suite 240
New York, NY 10011
USA
enslow.com

Published in 2018 by Enslow Publishing, LLC.
101 W. 23rd Street, Suite 240, New York, NY 10011

Library of Congress Cataloging-in-Publication Data

Names: Gordon, Sherri Mabry.
Title: Surviving a first breakup / Sherri Mabry Gordon.
Description: New York : Enslow Publishing, 2018. | Series: Teen survival guide | Includes bibliographical references and index. | Audience: Grades 7–12.
Identifiers: ISBN 9780766091924 (library bound) | ISBN 9780766093638 (pbk.) | ISBN 9780766093645 (6 pack)
Subjects: LCSH: Dating (Social customs)—Juvenile literature. | Separation (Psychology)—Juvenile literature. | Interpersonal relations—Juvenile literature.
Classification: LCC HQ801.G67 2018 | DDC 306.73—dc23

Printed in the United States of America

To Our Readers: We have done our best to make sure all websites in this book were active and appropriate when we went to press. However, the author and the publisher have no control over and assume no liability for the material available on those websites or on any websites they may link to. Any comments or suggestions can be sent by email to customerservice@enslow.com.

Photo Credits: Cover SpeedKingz/Shutterstock.com; p. 5 Dragana Gordic/Shutterstock.com; p. 6 pixelheadphoto digitalskillet/Shutterstock.com; p. 9 MJTH/Shutterstock.com; p. 10 fizkes/Shutterstock.com; p. 13 Crystal Home/Shutterstock.com; pp. 18, 24, 34 Antonio Guillem/Shutterstock.com; p. 21 digitalskillet/Shutterstock.com; p. 26 oneinchpunch/Shutterstock.com; p. 29 Andy Dean Photography/Shutterstock.com; p. 37 © iStockphoto.com/ClarkandCompany; p. 41 © iStockphoto.com/Weekend Images Inc.; p. 42 Dean Drobot/Shutterstock.com; cover and interior pages graphic elements © iStockphoto.com/marigold_88 (waves), Milos Djapovic/Shutttesrock.com (rough texture), Miloje/Shutterstock.com.com (circles).

CONTENTS

INTRODUCTION..4

CHAPTER **ONE**
WHY RELATIONSHIPS FAIL...8

CHAPTER **TWO**
BREAKING UP IS HARD TO DO 17

CHAPTER **THREE**
GETTING OVER GETTING DUMPED.........................23

CHAPTER **FOUR**
ADVICE FOR THOSE DOING THE DUMPING.........33

CHAPTER **FIVE**
LETTING GO AND MOVING ON 39

GLOSSARY..45
FURTHER READING 46
INDEX 48

INTRODUCTION

It was 2 a.m. on Christmas morning when Claire received the text message: "We need to talk." She knew what those words meant and pressed her boyfriend for answers. Eventually, what she discovered was that he wanted to exchange Christmas gifts and then break up. But if the relationship was ending, she decided it was better for it to happen right then rather than allow it to impact Christmas Day.

"At first, I wasn't too sad. I was more angry," Claire explains. "It made me mad that he did it on Christmas and through a text message. To me, that made him a coward."

Looking back, Claire says she saw the signs that he was not good for her and that the two were not compatible. For instance, her ex often made fun of other people. And while his words would bother her, she says she just "shoved it away" or brushed off his rudeness.

"I realized that you have to pay attention to your gut," she says. "If red flags are popping up everywhere, chances are they mean something. In my case, his comments truly were rude and I should not have ignored the fact that it bothered me."

Many teens break up with their boyfriend or girlfriend through text messages. But experts recommend that breakups be handled face to face.

She also says it's important to listen to your family and friends. "A lot of times they see things that you do not see," she says. "So if they say something like 'Hey, I think that he is mean to people or a little narcissistic,' then pay attention to that. They are not saying it to hurt you, but to tell you what is actually going on."

When you're having issues in your relationship, it's always a good idea to get input from friends and family. They often see things that you do not. They can also provide advice, support, and comfort.

Tyler's experience was similar to Claire's. He also broke up with his girlfriend on Christmas Day. But his breakup had been in the works for quite some time. After all, Tyler and Dana struggled with trust issues in their relationship and had been arguing constantly for months, especially about her ex-boyfriend. Finally, Tyler had enough of the lies and trust issues.

The toughest thing about the breakup was feeling like there was never any closure, Tyler explains. "I never got to share my feelings. She would twist and turn things until it was always my fault. She lied about going out with her ex-boyfriend but then made it seem like I was a terrible person for even finding out."

Today, Tyler says he has learned that he really needs to take things slow and figure out what he wants in a person. Meanwhile, Claire offers this advice: "Your life is not over. This is not the only person that is ever going to be interested in you. You will have other boyfriends or girlfriends. So don't dwell on the fact that this one relationship didn't work out. Figure out why it ended and then move on.""

CHAPTER ONE

WHY RELATIONSHIPS FAIL

Breaking up is messy. Not only can it feel like someone stabbed a nail in your heart, you may also struggle to make sense of the loss you are feeling. And while you cannot imagine that anyone has ever felt the way you do, what you are feeling is actually pretty normal.

Almost everyone experiences a painful breakup at least once in their lifetime. And although it might feel like your life is over, it's not. You will survive.

UNDERSTANDING WHY YOUR RELATIONSHIP ENDED

In the beginning, it is easy to dwell on what went wrong. Obsessing over every little argument and disagreement, you try to analyze what you could have done differently. While it is

Breakups are not easy to go through. But if you focus on moving forward, instead of what could have been, you'll be feeling better in no time.

tempting to relive the past over and over again, instead take a realistic look at what went wrong. Once you recognize where the problems were, you will be better equipped to keep it from happening in your next relationship. And there will be a next relationship!

Overall, there are seven primary reasons that teen relationships do not work out. These include everything from lack of attention to relationship abuse. If you are really

Disagreements are normal in a relationship. But when there are more bad times than good, it may be time to reevaluate the health of the relationship.

honest with yourself, you will be able to see that one or more of these reasons led to the demise of your relationship.

Different priorities. Maintaining a relationship takes work. But if you and your ex are like other teens, you're busy. School, extracurricular activities, work, and family commitments take time. It can be hard to make room in your life for a relationship. At your age, that is OK. This does not mean that you do not matter. You do. It is just that the focus is elsewhere right now.

Poor communication. Communication issues are probably the biggest deal breakers for a relationship. Aside from not talking about what you want from the relationship, you or your partner might also struggle with active listening and being assertive.

Lack of maturity. Let's face it, in your teen years you are still growing and learning about new things. This growth is what leads to maturity. And while you may be mature in some parts of your life, there are still some areas where you might need to grow. As a result, some teen relationships come to an end because one or both of you lack the maturity to stay together. This is not always a negative thing. This is an experience thing.

Different expectations. Sometimes couples discover that they have different goals and expectations. For instance, one person may want to go away to college and the other may want to stay in town. Or maybe one of you wants to focus on school activities while the other prefers to have a job. Whatever your expectations, this can lead to conflict when it comes to making decisions and spending time together.

Lack of trust. Lack of trust can be very harmful to a relationship. Without trust, a relationship will no longer feel safe or secure. There are any number of things that can cause trust issues, like jealousy, possessiveness, cheating, not being reliable, lack of support, and playing games.

Abuse. Everyone deserves to be treated with respect and dignity. But when one person in a relationship is abusive, the relationship will not survive. Regardless of whether or not the abuse includes verbal insults and name-calling or physical threats and violence, it is unhealthy. What's more, it is hurting both of you in the process.

Incompatibility. In the beginning of the relationship, you may have felt like you and your partner had a lot in common. But the more time you spent together, you started to realize that you had different values and

When a relationship ends, take some time to think about what went wrong. Make sure you look for mistakes you made, as well as your partner. This way you can make wiser choices next time.

beliefs. Consequently, you seemed to clash a lot. While there is some truth to the fact that opposites attract, polar opposites do not always mesh well together.

TOP MISTAKES TEENS MAKE IN RELATIONSHIPS

Sometimes teen relationships end because one or both partners have an unhealthy habit they need to break. Take a look at the top unhealthy habits teens have that can lead to a relationship's end. Do you see yourself or your partner in this list? If you do, it is time to work on making a few changes before you start dating again.

Mistake #1: Relying on your partner for happiness. Expecting your partner to make you happy all the time puts too much pressure on him or her. What's more, it is not your partner's responsibility. Only you have the power to control your feelings.

Mistake #2: Giving in to the green-eyed monster. While feeling jealous from time to time is normal, it is not healthy to allow this emotion to take over. If you're prone to snooping around and checking up on your partner, you may be letting jealousy get the best of you. Even if your partner is being unfaithful, do not let your jealousy control you. Instead, talk calmly about the issue, and if he or she continues to be unfaithful, consider ending the relationship.

Mistake #3: Being a people pleaser. If you always put your feelings and desires aside to make someone else happy, that is people pleasing, and it is not healthy. What's more, your partner will learn to ignore what you want. Eventually, you may feel taken for granted and underappreciated.

Mistake #4: Being demanding, controlling, and selfish. This behavior is the opposite of people pleasing. Instead of trying to please your partner all the time, you expect him or her to be available to you all the time to do what you want. The selfish partner always chooses the restaurant, the movie, the party, and so on. In other words, you expect your partner to spend every free moment with you on your terms. And when he or she does not, you throw a fit. There is very rarely a compromise. What can eventually happen is that your partner will start to lie and sneak around to avoid hanging out with you or will eventually get fed up.

Mistake #5: Being critical. While it is important to be honest in a relationship, being too blunt about your partner's shortcomings communicates that he or she doesn't measure up. Not only will this slowly destroy your partner's self-esteem, but you also may be unknowingly pushing him or her away.

Mistake #6: Carrying around emotional baggage. This mistake happens when teens have not dealt with their past breakups or other problems, either from home, school, or elsewhere, in a healthy way. They then carry these unresolved issues and feelings into the next relationship. For this reason, it is very important that you learn how to let go of your negative emotions and move on. It will be the healthiest way to survive a breakup.

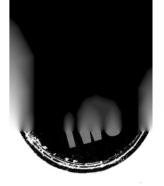

BREAKING UP IS HARD TO DO

Anytime you have to give up something you love, whether it is chocolate, social media, or even your phone, it is hard to do. Giving up the "love of your life" is no different. In fact, it is normal to be heartbroken when you break up. No one is ever happy to let go of a person who played such a big part in his or her life. So when the relationship comes to an end, it hurts. A lot.

At first, you might feel numb or even try to deny that the breakup really happened. Then, you might feel really angry. How dare your ex treat you like that, right? You may even try to convince your ex to get back together. But once you realize the breakup is really happening, you might feel very blue.

Even though it feels like an emotional roller coaster, this is all actually pretty normal. In fact, what you are experiencing has been labeled by doctors as "the cycle of grief."

It is normal to feel a wide variety of emotions when you break up —everything from anger to frustration, sadness to loneliness. You must allow yourself to feel these emotions—and work through them.

THE CYCLE OF GRIEF

A doctor in Switzerland, Elisabeth Kubler-Ross, was the first to highlight the grief cycle in her book *On Death and Dying*. Since then, people have realized that it's not just the terminally ill who go through a cycle of grief, but anyone who has gotten bad news. That means even you will go through a cycle of grief after breaking up.

To help you better understand what you might experience, here are seven phases of the grief cycle.

- Shock—Disbelieving that the relationship is ending
- Denial—Trying to avoid or denying the bad news
- Anger—Releasing emotions and frustrations
- Bargaining—Trying to keep the relationship from ending by begging the person to stay or trying to win the person back
- Depression—Realizing that the relationship is truly over despite your efforts as sadness sets in
- Testing—Exploring different ideas on how to move on
- Acceptance—Finding a way to finally let go

Although the shock phase and the testing phase are not part of Kubler-Ross's initial cycle of grief, some experts include these phases to help you understand how you might transition from one phase to another. What's more, you may move quickly through a few of the phases but then spend a little more time in some of the others. Everyone is different. And even though it may seem like there is no light at the end of the tunnel, with time and a little hard work, you will start to feel better.

SINGING THE BLUES

It is normal to feel sad after a breakup. In fact, during those first days you may feel so much grief and sadness that you are not sure how you are going to survive. But, little by little and day by day, your sadness will begin to lift and you will start accepting that the relationship is over. And that is a good thing.

If you seem to be getting sadder each day or feel like you have fallen into a black hole, this is not normal sadness. It is especially worrisome if you no longer are interested in doing the things you once loved, have no appetite, want to sleep all day, and cannot even bring yourself to shower.

If any of this is happening to you, tell a parent or another trusted adult. You may be suffering from depression and need to be evaluated by a doctor. This is not something you want to hide; nor is it anything to be embarrassed about. With the right treatment, you will be back to your old self in no time.

GIVE YOUR HEART A BREAK

When you break up, remember that while you cannot keep the relationship from ending, you can control your response to its end. Here are some comparisons about what is healthy and what is not.

Talking to someone about what you're feeling can help you to make sense of your situation. Do not be afraid to ask a parent, a teacher, or a counselor for advice.

- It's healthy to talk to a few close friends about what you are going through and how you feel. But it is unhealthy to involve your friends in the breakup process where they are relaying information or taking sides. Things get messy when too many people weigh in on what's going on during the breakup.

21

- It is normal to feel angry when your relationship ends. But it is unhealthy to express this anger in destructive ways such as destroying property or plotting revenge. If you have a lot of pent-up anger, try exercising or journaling to release some steam.
- It is acceptable to change your relationship status online. But it is unhealthy to cyberstalk your ex, subtweet about him, or post passive-aggressive comments about your relationship. In fact, you may want to stay off social media for awhile until your heart heals.

Overall, the best way to deal with the wide range of emotions you might be feeling is to allow yourself to experience them. Be honest with yourself about how you are feeling and make sure you choose healthy and constructive ways to deal with your pain and heartbreak.

CHAPTER THREE

GETTING OVER GETTING DUMPED

Those first days following your breakup, your focus should be on healing your heart. It's important to take care of yourself. Remember, that no matter how bad you feel right now, you are going to slowly but surely begin to feel better.

HEALING YOUR ACHY BREAKY HEART

Getting over a broken relationship is a lot like getting over the flu. You need plenty of rest. Eating healthy, exercising, taking it easy, and reducing your commitments are other things you can do to mend your broken heart. The point is that you must take good care of yourself. This is not the time to stop sleeping and eating. Instead, focus on getting better so that you can move on with your life. Here are some other self-care tips that will help you mend your heart.

When getting over a breakup, it is important to take time for yourself every day. Have a cup of coffee, go for a walk, or listen to some music. Do something that will help you relax and calm your nerves.

Take time each day for yourself. It is not selfish to think about yourself in those first few weeks after a breakup. Schedule some time every day to do something you find relaxing and calming. For instance, you could go for a walk, take a hot bath, listen to music, savor a hot cup of tea—anything that will soothe your frazzled nerves. And if you need to, cry it out. Some people try not to cry when a relationship ends. But research shows that crying is actually good for you. So be sure to let your tears flow. It is not a sign of weakness, but instead a way to cleanse your heart and soul of the pain you are feeling. As a result, you should never feel ashamed for crying. Bottling up your emotions doesn't make you a strong person. Your feelings will have to go somewhere. So it is better to let it out now than deal with an explosion down the road.

If you feel up to it, make a list of your ex's annoying qualities. When you break up with someone, it is very easy to remember only the good things, which intensifies the loss you are feeling. Instead, try writing down all the incompatibilities and problems of your relationship. Doing so will make it much easier to let go. It also will help you see that there is likely a better match for you out there.

Create a routine and stick to it. It is not uncommon for a breakup to disrupt your life. After all, breaking up with someone creates chaos in your life, and, remember, you are no longer spending time with your partner. Having a regular routine and sticking to it will provide the structure you need when you feel like you are falling apart. And try to avoid "escaping." When you are going through a breakup, it is tempting to do anything to relieve your pain. For some people this might mean using food, alcohol, drugs, or hooking up to forget about the hurt and confusion. Aside

Sometimes the best way to get over a breakup is to laugh a little. Make sure you find time to have fun with your friends. You will feel much better if you do.

from being unhealthy, these coping strategies only mask the pain. They do not make it go away. And when you get up the next day, you still have to deal with your broken heart.

Instead, why not try and laugh a little. There is truth in the saying "laughter is the best medicine." So make sure you indulge a little. Watch a comedy or call your funniest friend.

You can also read a funny book, watch a favorite sitcom with friends, or download silly cat videos. If you can laugh a little, your brain (and your heart) will recognize that life is not over, even though it may feel like it.

Be sure to talk about your feelings. It is normal to have lots of conflicting emotions. One day you might feel anger and resentment, the next day you might experience sadness, fear, and confusion. All of these feelings are normal. Try sharing them with a close friend or a trusted adult. Just knowing that others are aware of your feelings will make you feel less alone with your pain. It also is very healing to get things out. This will help you focus on moving forward. The problem with negative feelings is that they can sometimes cause you to get stuck. Remember your goal is to keep moving forward so that you do not feel pain any longer. If you keep cycling through the same thoughts and memories, it is time to disrupt the cycle and think about something else. You do not want to dwell on your negative feelings or overanalyze your situation. Giving too much time to your negative thoughts robs you of energy and prevents you from moving on.

DON'T GO BREAKING YOUR HEART

When you are going through a breakup, it is easy to become so overwhelmed by your emotions that you make unfortunate mistakes. Some examples include calling or texting your ex in the middle of the night or finding excuses to see him or her. While it may be tempting to do any number of these things, this is not going to help you feel better. In fact, you will likely feel much worse. Here are the top mistakes to avoid when getting over a breakup.

- **Don't ask questions that you don't want to know the answers to.** As tempting as it might be to find out if your ex is dating someone new, knowing this answer is not going to make you feel better. Staying off social media will help with this.

- **Don't try to rekindle the relationship.** Bringing closure to the relationship is going to be impossible if you keep hoping the two of you will get back together. Try to accept the fact that it didn't work out and honor your ex's request for space.

- **Don't call, text, email, Skype, or reach out to your ex.** By all means, do not call your ex and cry about how brokenhearted you are. Likewise, do not send long emails or leave rambling voicemail messages explaining why the two of you belong together. Not only is this approach usually ineffective, but those moments of weakness could also be embarrassing for you later. Remember, closure happens more quickly when you minimize contact with your ex.

- **Don't post about the breakup on social media.** Many times, teens will tweet or post about how much

Put your smartphone away after a breakup. Avoid calling, texting, and posting on social media when you are upset. Most of the time, you will regret using your cell phone while emotional. Journal instead!

their heart hurts without ever mentioning their ex. The problem is that everyone at school probably already knows that the two of you broke up. So your subtle tweet is not really so subtle. It will only open you up to gossip and rumors. It is best to stay off of social media until you start feeling better.

- **Don't personalize the loss.** Do not blame yourself for the breakup. Sometimes you can create unnecessary heartache for yourself if you assume there is something wrong with you or that the breakup is your fault. Trying to attach blame to yourself (or to your ex) is not helpful to the healing process. It is much healthier to place the blame where it belongs: on conflicting needs and incompatible personalities.

- **Don't isolate yourself.** As tempting as it might be to cut yourself off from the rest of the world, this is not healthy. Instead, try to hang out with your friends even when you do not feel like it. You cannot heal properly if you do not have any human contact.

- **Don't lose faith in dating.** Because you are in a lot of pain right after the breakup, it may be tempting to assume that no one is worth dating. But swearing off dating indefinitely could be robbing you of meeting someone great down the road.

- **Don't threaten to kill yourself.** Threatening suicide is never a good idea. Even if you are just being dramatic and have no intention of ever following through, suicide is a serious situation and should never be taken lightly. If you are truly having thoughts of suicide, you need to talk to a trusted adult right away. No breakup is ever worth losing your life over.

SUICIDE WARNING SIGNS

If you, or someone you know, displays any of these signs, contact a trusted adult right away. Or call the National Suicide Prevention Lifeline at 800-273-8255.

- Talks about suicide
- Makes comments about no one caring if they are gone
- Has a preoccupation with death and dying
- Says they feel hopeless, helpless, or worthless
- Does things that are out of character
- Loses interest in favorite activities
- Takes lots of risks or is self-destructive
- Starts giving away stuff, even things that are really special to them
- Writes notes or calls people to tell them how much they love them

YOU WILL SURVIVE

Although it may not feel like it right now, you will survive this breakup. And you might just get stronger in the process. Studies show that surviving a breakup is easier than you might think.

In fact, one study found that most people overestimate how bad a breakup will be and how long it will take to get over it. They just do not realize how resilient they truly are. What's more, the study found that many people were back to "normal" at about the two-month mark.

When you think about it, that's not a very long time. So the next time you are feeling miserable about breaking up with the love of your life, just remind yourself that in about two months, you will wonder what the fuss was all about.

CHAPTER FOUR

ADVICE FOR THOSE DOING THE DUMPING

There is never a good time to break up with someone. Ever. What's more, staying with someone because you are too afraid to end it is downright unfair. It is a lot meaner to stay with someone because you are a coward or too lazy than it is to break up with them. And it is even worse to stay with someone because you pity him or her. Breaking up is kind of like ripping off a bandage. You have to just do it.

If you are in a relationship that isn't working out and you are thinking about ending it, below are some things you'll want to consider first. And while it will still be uncomfortable and painful for both of you, if you handle the breakup with compassion and respect, you can walk away with no regrets.

If you are considering breaking up with your boyfriend or girlfriend, sit down and talk about it. Make an effort to handle the breakup with compassion and respect, and you can walk away with no regrets.

SO YOU'RE READY
TO BREAK UP

Talk to someone first. This is especially important if you have been dating the person for awhile. Your friends and family members can provide you with insight into the relationship that you may not be able to see. What's more, this information can confirm that breaking up is for the best. Be sure to talk to someone who won't gossip about your relationship; you want to be the one to tell your partner the news, not for him or her to hear about it from someone else.

Always break up in person. Sure, it is hard to break up with someone in person. After all, you have to see the pain and shock on the person's face and know that you are the one causing it. But it has to be done. Of course it is much easier to break up over a text message. But that is rude, and you owe this person who cares about you more than that. Do the right thing and break up face-to-face. The only exception to this rule involves breaking up with someone who is toxic or abusive.

Do not break up in public. Breaking up with someone in a public place is unfair to the person on the receiving end. Who wants an audience when their heart is being ripped out? Have respect for the person and do it in private. This way, he or she can shed a tear or two without feeling humiliated by having an audience.

Never make a scene. Breaking up is painful for both of you. But try to keep your emotions in check. Yelling insults or hurling accusations during the breakup is not called for. Keep your explanation short and simple. There is no need to drag it out. Say what you need to say and allow your partner to ask a few questions. But try to avoid a long, drawn-out breakup.

Do not try to make the other person feel better. In other words, avoid the classic "It's not you, it's me" statement. And certainly do not hug or kiss the person to try to make him or her feel better. Once the relationship is over, you have lost the right to do that. Plus, it confuses the person whose heart is newly broken.

Cut all contact. After you have broken up and met to return each other's things, do not have any more contact for awhile. This is really important. Research shows that limiting contact can actually help both of you recover much more quickly.

Don't judge or blame anyone. Focus on the fact that you are not compatible and refrain from casting blame. The relationship didn't work out. There is no need to list off all the terrible things that your partner did.

HOW TO END TOXIC RELATIONSHIPS

If you are in an abusive relationship, breaking up requires extra thought and consideration because you must consider your safety. No one should stay in an abusive relationship. Usually, the abuse escalates over time and gets worse. Remind yourself that things are not going to get better, even if your partner promises to never hurt you again.

When it comes to ending a toxic relationship, it is usually recommended to have a safety plan in place. This means telling other people you are planning to break up with your partner. It is important that people know what is happening so that they can help keep you safe. Unfortunately, abuse often escalates at the time of a breakup because the abusive partner realizes that he or she is losing control over you.

This is a time when it is acceptable to break up over the phone or in a public place with a few friends or adults nearby. Your safety should be your top concern when ending the relationship.

Breaking up with an abusive person is the one time it is appropriate to break up over the phone or through text. Controlling partners are the most dangerous when they think they are losing you.

Last, once the relationship has ended cut off all contact with your ex. Block his or her number from your phone. Unfriend him or her on social media and make sure your accounts are private. Do not agree to meet for any reason, even if your ex threatens suicide. Instead, call the police and let them know that your ex is threatening suicide. They are better equipped to handle those situations than you are. You also do not owe them an explanation for the breakup, and you are not equipped to save your ex's life.

Remember, "no" is a complete sentence, according to Barrie Levy, author of *In Love and In Danger: A Teen's Guide to Breaking Free of Abusive Relationships*. You do not have to explain anything to your ex. In fact, the less contact you have with him or her, the better it is for you.

TYING UP LOOSE ENDS

Everyone goes into a relationship with good intentions. No one really wants to hurt someone. But relationships are messy, and it is not uncommon to come away feeling hurt and betrayed, even if you were the one doing the dumping. The important thing is that you learn from the mistakes and move on.

Think about the relationship after you end it. Reflect on your actions and behaviors while you were dating and try to think about what you could do differently next time around. Ask yourself what you learned. You might want to avoid rushing into another relationship right away. Being single is not a bad thing, especially when you are a teenager. Having time to try new things, invest in yourself, and discover who you are is a vital part of growing up. Take time to enjoy it. It won't last forever.

LETTING GO AND MOVING ON

A uthor C. S. Lewis once said, "Getting over a painful experience is much like crossing the monkey bars. You have to let go at some point in order to move forward." The same is true of a breakup. If you want to move on to a healthier, happier place, you are going to have to let go at some point.

GETTING STARTED

When trying to move on after you've had your heart broken, you want to be sure you are making the right decisions. Sometimes teens can make mistakes that keep them locked in emotional limbo, and they are never really able to move on. Here are the top three things you should avoid doing.

LET'S BE FRIENDS. NOT!

Sometimes, people think they can at least be friends with their significant other. But that is hard to do, especially if one of you still wants the relationship to work. It is actually better for you to have little to no contact with your ex. Even if you think you could be friends in the future, it is better to make a clean break. Staying in contact with an ex keeps you emotionally tied to the person and you are never really able to move on.

DON'T RUSH INTO A REBOUND

Rebound relationships don't always work out. Bouncing from one relationship to another doesn't allow you time to learn from your mistakes. As a result, you will likely keep having the same relationship issues. Take some time for yourself without a boyfriend or girlfriend at your side. You don't want to wind up with the same type of person over and over again.

STOP LOOKING BACK

One way to keep yourself moving on through a painful breakup is to plan for the future. Put things on your calendar. Doing so keeps your eyes on the days ahead and not on the past. For instance, if there is a concert you want to see, put the ticket sale date on your calendar. Is there a family vacation in the future? Mark it down. You can also plan things with friends, like shopping trips, movie nights, coffee dates, and more. If you plan little things every week, this keeps you moving forward rather than staying in one place, thinking about your ex and what he or she is doing.

Making future plans and putting them on a calendar can give you something to look forward to. It also helps you focus on the future instead of looking to the past.

TAKING A CLOSER LOOK

In order to truly move on from a broken relationship, you have to be able to see not only what happened, but also what part you played in the relationship's demise. The point of this exercise is not to dwell on who is to blame for the relationship ending. Nor is it about beating yourself up for making mistakes. Instead, it is a time to be honest with yourself so that you can grow and learn from your breakup.

After a breakup, take a closer look at issues you need to work on. If you are honest about your shortcomings, you will see what needs to change and ultimately be in a better place for your next relationship.

What's more, you will learn more about yourself, how you communicate with others, and the issues you need to work on. If you are truly honest with yourself, you will be able to see what needs to change going forward. Empower yourself to make better choices next time. Assuming that you are perfect and your ex is the only one with issues will keep you stuck repeating the same patterns of behavior. Here are some questions to ask yourself.

THE POWER OF POSITIVE THINKING

So your relationship ended. That doesn't mean that your entire life is doomed. It also doesn't mean that you will never have another date in your life. The world is full of guys and girls, and there is someone out there for you. Even though it may not seem like it right now, someday you will meet someone who will make you even happier than your ex did.

The key is to stay positive. Often this begins with positive self-talk. In other words, don't say negative things to yourself like, "I'm a loser," "No one will ever want me," or "I can't seem to do anything right." These are harmful statements, and they are simply not true. Instead, replace your negative self-talk with positive thoughts. Remind yourself that you are a good person with a lot to offer the world. Say things like, "I am a good friend" and "I am loyal and dependable." Positive thinking and statements reaffirm your worth and identity and give you a greater overall sense of well-being.

Look back on the relationship. Write down what your biggest issues were while you were dating. What did you disagree about? How did you contribute to these issues? How can you be different next time?

Think about your ex. What qualities or characteristics were unhealthy or not suited to your personality? Do you tend to choose this type of person on a regular basis? Why do you think that is?

Write down the type of person you would like to date in the future. What type of person do you think is best suited for you? What can you change to pick more compatible dating partners in the future?

Consider how you react to stress and deal with conflict in a relationship. Is there anything that you should change?

Examine yourself and what you were like while you were dating your ex. Do you like who you were? Would you say that you were confident or insecure? How were you emotionally? Did you respond to situations in a healthy way? Or did you struggle with control, jealousy, or envy? How can you change in the future?

LITTLE MISS (OR MISTER) MOVIN' ON

As your heart heals, there will be good days and there will be bad days. But if you keep focusing on moving forward you will be fine. Remember, when you let go of your ex in a healthy way, you will be in a better place emotionally. What's more, you will be ready for all the new dating opportunities that await you.

Don't miss out on what lies ahead by keeping one foot in the past. Instead, focus on putting one foot in front of the other and walk right into the future that is waiting for you. You will feel so much better if you do.

GLOSSARY

abusive Using cruel words or physical violence, like hitting.

assertive Being bold and confident in how one talks and acts.

closure A feeling of finality, often comforting.

constructive Helping to improve.

demise A death or ending.

evaluate To examine something closely to determine how much it is worth.

incompatible Not able to be together in a pleasing, harmonious way.

narcissistic Love for oneself, often to the exclusion of others.

primary First and most important.

priority Something that gets attention first, before other alternatives.

rekindle To stir something up again, like excitement.

resilience The ability to get over something difficult .

self-talk The act of talking to yourself, either out loud or in your head.

STD A sexually transmitted disease, a disease you get from sexual contact with another person.

FURTHER READING

BOOKS

Becker-Phelps Leslie. *Insecure in Love: How Anxious Attachment Can Make You Feel Jealous, Needy, and Worried*. Oakland, CA: New Harbinger Publications, 2014.

Bennett, Joan, and David Bennett. *The Teen Popularity Handbook: Make Friends, Get Dates, and Become Bully-Proof*. Columbus, OH: Theta Hill Press, 2014.

Buddenberg, Laura, and Alecia Montgomery. *Dating: 10 Tips for a Successful Relationship*. Boys Town, NE: Boys Town Press, 2013.

Eastham, Chad. *The Truth About Breaking Up, Making Up, and Moving On*. Nashville, TN: Thomas Nelson, 2013.

Van Dijk, Sheri. *Relationship Skills 101 for Teens: Your Guide to Dealing with Daily Drama, Stress, and Difficult Emotions*. Oakland, CA: Instant Help, 2015.

WEBSITES

Girls Health

www.girlshealth.gov/relationships/dating/index.html
A comprehensive, interactive guide to healthy dating, with quizzes and more.

Healthy Relationships

www.youngwomenshealth.org/2011/06/02/healthy-relationships
Run by the Center for Young Women's Health, you'll find real-life advice and handy tips for keeping your relationship healthy—or deciding to end it.

Safe Teens

www.safeteens.org/relationships
This site provides lots of information on all kinds of relationships and more serious info, too, about sexting, STDs, and more.

INDEX

A

abuse/abusive relationships, 12,
    26–37
acceptance, 19, 20, 28
anger, as part of cycle of grief, 19

B

bargaining, 19
breaking up with someone, how to,
    34–37

C

cheating, 14–15
crying, benefits of, 25
cycle of grief, 17, 18–19

D

denial, 19
depression, 19, 20

E

emotions, sharing them with friends,
    27

F

friendship, trying to maintain with
    an ex, 39–40
future, planning for, 40

I

incompatibility, 12, 14, 25

J

jealousy, 14–15

L

laughter, 26–27

M

mistakes, common ones made in
    relationships, 14–16

P

people pleasers, 15
positive thinking, 43
postbreakup behavior, healthy
    versus unhealthy, 20–22, 28–30

R

rebound relationships, 40
reflection, on why a relationship
    ended, 41–44
relationship failures, seven primary
    reasons for, 10–11

S

self-care tips, 23–27
shock, 19
suicide, 30, 31, 37

T

testing, 19
trust issues, 6, 12